FORWARD/COMMENTARY

The National Institute of Standards and Technology (NIST) is a measurement standards laboratory, and a non-regulatory agency of the **United States Department of Commerce**. Its mission is to promote innovation and industrial competitiveness. Founded in 1901, as the National Bureau of Standards, NIST was formed with the mandate to provide standard weights and measures, and to serve as the national physical laboratory for the United States. With a world-class measurement and testing laboratory encompassing a wide range of areas of computer science, mathematics, statistics, and systems engineering, NIST's cybersecurity program supports its overall mission to promote U.S. innovation and industrial competitiveness by advancing measurement science, standards, and related technology through research and development in ways that enhance economic security and improve our quality of life.

The need for cybersecurity standards and best practices that address interoperability, usability and privacy has been shown to be critical for the nation. NIST's cybersecurity programs seek to enable greater development and application of practical, innovative security technologies and methodologies that enhance the country's ability to address current and future computer and information security challenges.

The cybersecurity publications produced by NIST cover a wide range of cybersecurity concepts that are carefully designed to work together to produce a holistic approach to cybersecurity primarily for government agencies and constitute the best practices used by industry. This holistic strategy to cybersecurity covers the gamut of security subjects from development of secure encryption standards for communication and storage of information while at rest to how best to recover from a cyber-attack.

Why buy a book you can download for free?   We print this so you don't have to.

Some are available only in electronic media. Some online docs are missing pages or barely legible.

We at 4th Watch Publishing are former government employees, so we know how government employees actually use the standards. When a new standard is released, an engineer prints it out, punches holes and puts it in a 3-ring binder. While this is not a big deal for a 5 or 10-page document, many NIST documents are over 100 pages and printing a large document is a time-consuming effort. So, an engineer that's paid $75 an hour is spending hours simply printing out the tools needed to do the job. That's time that could be better spent doing engineering. We publish these documents so engineers can focus on what they were hired to do – engineering. It's much more cost-effective to just order the latest version from Amazon.com

If there is a standard you would like published, let us know. Our web site is www.usgovpub.com

Many of our titles are available as ePubs for Kindle, iPad, Nook, remarkable, BOOX, and Sony eReaders.

Why buy an eBook when you can access data on a website for free? HYPERLINKS

Yes, many books are available as a PDF, but not all PDFs are bookmarked? Do you really want to search a 6,500-page PDF document manually? Load our copy onto your Kindle, PC, iPad, Android Tablet, Nook, or iPhone (download the FREE kindle App from the APP Store) and you have an easily searchable copy. Most devices will allow you to easily navigate an ePub to any Chapter. Note that there is a distinction between a Table of Contents and "Page Navigation". Page Navigation refers to a different sort of Table of Contents. Not one appearing as a page in the book, but one that shows up on the device itself when the reader accesses the navigation feature. Readers can click on a navigation link to jump to a Chapter or Subchapter. Once there, most devices allow you to "pinch and zoom" in or out to easily read the text. (Unfortunately, downloading the free sample file at Amazon.com does not include this feature. You have to buy a copy to get that functionality, but as inexpensive as eBooks are, it's worth it.) Kindle allows you to do word search and Page Flip (temporary place holder takes you back when you want to go back and check something). Visit **www.usgovpub.com** to learn more.

SECURING TELEHEALTH REMOTE PATIENT MONITORING ECOSYSTEM

Cybersecurity for the Healthcare Sector

Andrea Arbelaez
National Cybersecurity Center of Excellence
National Institute of Standards and Technology

Ronnie Daldos
Kevin Littlefield
Sue Wang
David Weitzel
The MITRE Corporation

DRAFT
November 2018
hit_nccoe@nist.gov

The National Cybersecurity Center of Excellence (NCCoE), a part of the National Institute of Standards and Technology (NIST), is a collaborative hub where industry organizations, government agencies, and academic institutions work together to address businesses' most pressing cybersecurity challenges. Through this collaboration, the NCCoE develops modular, easily adaptable example cybersecurity solutions demonstrating how to apply standards and best practices using commercially available technology. To learn more about the NCCoE, visit http://www.nccoe.nist.gov. To learn more about NIST, visit http://www.nist.gov.

This document describes a particular problem that is relevant across the healthcare sector. NCCoE cybersecurity experts will address this challenge through collaboration with members of the healthcare sector and vendors of cybersecurity solutions. The resulting reference design will detail an approach that can be used by healthcare delivery organizations (HDOs).

ABSTRACT

HDOs are leveraging a combination of telehealth capabilities, such as remote patient monitoring (RPM) and videoconferencing, to treat patients in their homes. These modalities are used to treat numerous conditions, such as patients battling chronic illness or requiring post-operative monitoring. As the use of these capabilities continues to grow, it is important to ensure that the infrastructure supporting them can maintain the confidentiality, integrity, and availability of patient data, and to ensure the safety of patients. The goal of this project is to provide a practical solution for securing the telehealth RPM ecosystem. The project team will perform a risk assessment on a representative RPM ecosystem in the laboratory environment, apply the NIST Cybersecurity Framework and guidance based on medical device standards, and collaborate with industry and public partners. The project team will also create a reference design and a detailed description of the practical steps needed to implement a secure solution based on standards and best practices. This project will result in a freely available NIST Cybersecurity Practice Guide.

KEYWORDS

application programming interface (API); application security; cybersecurity; data privacy; data privacy and security risks; health delivery organization (HDO); remote patient monitoring (RPM); telehealth; user interface (UI)

DISCLAIMER

COMMENTS ON NCCoE DOCUMENTS

Organizations are encouraged to review all draft publications during public comment periods and provide feedback. All publications from NIST's National Cybersecurity Center of Excellence are available at http://www.nccoe.nist.gov.

Comments on this publication may be submitted to: hit-nccoe@nist.gov

Public comment period: November 19, 2018 to December 21, 2018

TABLE OF CONTENTS

1 EXECUTIVE SUMMARY

Purpose

This document defines a National Cybersecurity Center of Excellence (NCCoE) project focused on providing guidance and a reference architecture that address security and privacy risks to stakeholders leveraging telehealth and remote patient monitoring (RPM) capabilities. We are seeking feedback on this project.

Traditionally, patient monitoring systems have been deployed in healthcare facilities, in controlled environments. RPM, however, is different, in that monitoring equipment is deployed in the patient's home, which traditionally does not offer the same level of cybersecurity or physical-security control to prevent misuse or compromise. These RPM devices may leverage application programming interfaces (APIs) or rule engines developed by third parties that act as intermediaries between the patient and the healthcare provider. It is important to review the end-to-end architecture to determine whether security and privacy vulnerabilities exist and what security controls are required for proper cybersecurity of the RPM ecosystem.

While the field of telehealth is broad, a focus on the application of telehealth modalities involving third-party platform providers utilizing videoconferencing capabilities and leveraging cloud and internet technologies coupled with RPM mechanisms provides the NCCoE with an opportunity to develop practical recommendations. The intended audience for these recommendations consists of HDOs, patients, and third-party participants employing RPM products and services.

This project will result in a publicly available National Institute of Standards and Technology (NIST) Cybersecurity Practice Guide, a detailed implementation guide of the practical steps needed to implement a cybersecurity reference design that addresses this challenge.

Scope

The objective of this project is to demonstrate a proposed approach for improving the overall security in the RPM environment. This project will address cybersecurity concerns about having monitoring devices in patients' homes, including the use of the home network and patient-owned devices, such as smartphones, tablets, laptops, and home computers. This project will also identify cybersecurity measures that HDOs may consider when offering RPM with video telehealth capabilities. A proposed component list is provided in the High-Level Architecture section (Section 3).

Telehealth solutions are, by nature, an integration of disparate parties and environments. However, out of scope for this project are the risks and concerns specific to the third-party provider (i.e., the telehealth platform provider) that may be offering services that are cloud-hosted or that provide functionality through a software as a service (SaaS) model. Additionally, this project does not evaluate monitoring devices for vulnerabilities, flaws, or defects. The intent of this project is to provide practical guidance for the security control. The NCCoE does not evaluate medical device manufacturers.

While telehealth solutions may include software development kits (SDKs) and APIs, this project will not explore the secure software development practice in detail.

Assumptions

- Patient monitoring devices (e.g., blood pressure cuff, body mass index [BMI] / weight scale) may leverage Bluetooth or wireless communications to transmit telemetry data to the home monitoring application.

- The home monitoring application may be installed on a managed or unmanaged patient-owned mobile device.

- The home monitoring application may transmit telemetry data to the remote monitoring server via a cellular or Wi-Fi connection.

- The patient is in his or her home during the telehealth interaction (e.g., video, patient monitoring).

- Video telehealth interactions may leverage patient-owned devices or devices provided by the primary care facility.

- Clinicians participating in telehealth interactions are connected to the HDO's internal network via a secure virtual private network (VPN) by using a device managed by the HDO.

Background

The NCCoE recognizes the important role that telehealth capabilities play in the delivery of healthcare and has commenced research in telehealth, specifically RPM technologies. As the growth and popularity of telehealth capabilities accelerate, it is critical to evaluate the security and privacy risks associated with each identified use case. Once identified, security controls can be implemented to mitigate the security and privacy risks to the patient and other stakeholders.

The demand for telehealth capabilities continues to grow as stakeholders (e.g., patients; providers; payers; federal, state, and local governments) see the benefits that telehealth brings to improving the quality of patient care and the accessibility to healthcare. A 2017 Foley Telemedicine and Digital Health Survey found that, in just three years, respondents went from 87 percent not expecting most of their patients to be using telehealth services in 2017 to 75 percent offering or planning to offer telehealth services to their patients [1].

2 SCENARIO: REMOTE PATIENT MONITORING AND VIDEO TELEHEALTH

The scenario considered for this project involves RPM equipment deployed to the patient's home [2]. RPM equipment that may be provided to patients includes devices for blood pressure monitoring, heart rate monitoring, BMI/weight measurements, and glucose monitoring. An accompanying application may also be downloaded onto the patient-owned device and synced with the RPM equipment to enable the patient and healthcare provider to share data. Patients may also be able to initiate videoconferencing and/or communicate with the healthcare provider via email, text messaging, or chat sessions. Data may be transmitted across the patient's home network and routed across the public internet. Those transmissions may be relayed to a third-party platform provider that, in turn, routes the communications to the HDO. This process brings the patient and healthcare provider together, allowing for the delivery of the needed healthcare services in the comfort of the patient's home.

The following functions may be evaluated during this project:

- connectivity between monitoring devices and applications deployed to mobile devices (e.g., smartphones, tablets) or to patient workstations (e.g., laptops, desktops)
- ability for the application to transmit monitoring data to the HDO
- ability for the patient to interact with a point of contact to initiate care (This ability may be through a chat box, interacting with a live individual via videoconference.)
- ability for the monitoring data to be analyzed by the HDO to spot trends and to issue possible alerts to the clinician if the data suggests that there is an issue with the patient
- ability for the patient monitoring data to be shared remotely with the electronic health record system
- ability for the patient to initiate a videoconference session with a care team member through the telehealth application
- ability for the patient to receive and apply updates and patches for applications
- ability for the HDO to establish connectivity to the remote monitoring device to obtain direct patient telemetry data
- ability for the HDO to establish connectivity to the remote monitoring device to update the monitoring device configuration

3 HIGH-LEVEL ARCHITECTURE

Figure 3-1 shows the high-level architecture for RPM that uses a third-party telehealth platform provider. The high-level architecture addresses the scope noted in Section 1. The component list and the desired security characteristics are listed the subsections that follow.

For this project, two separate environments will be constructed: the HDO environment and the patient home setting.

The HDO infrastructure would adopt the deployments used in previous NCCoE healthcare projects [3], [4] that implement network zoning and layered defenses aligning to NIST Cybersecurity Framework functions. As this project develops, identity and access management (IdAM) controls will be identified. IdAM may be limited based on selected technologies, and those limitations are to be determined.

DRAFT

Figure 3-1: High-Level Architecture

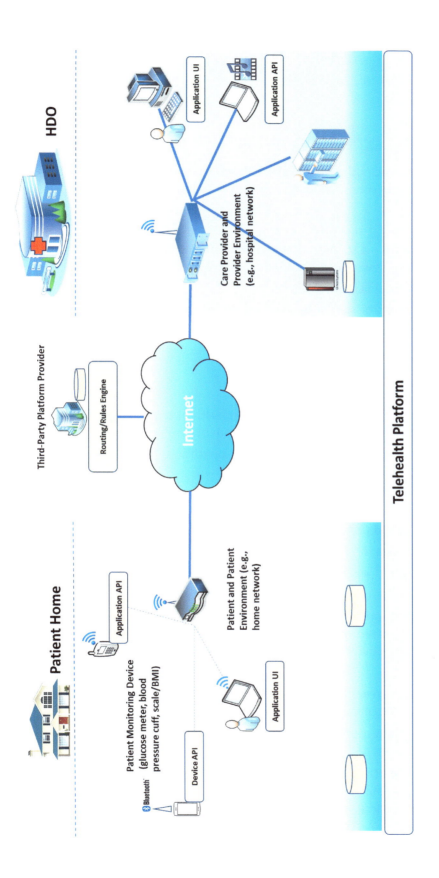

Component List

The NCCoE has a dedicated lab environment that includes the following features:

- network with machines using a directory service
- virtualization servers
- network switches
- remote access solution with Wi-Fi and a VPN

Collaboration partners (participating vendors) will need to provide specialized components and capabilities to realize this solution, including, but not limited to, those listed in the subsections below.

Components for RPM Technologies

- **Telehealth platform** – a solution that enables data and communication flow from the patient monitoring device to the home monitoring device to the care providers
  - internet-based communications
    - transmission of telemetry data
    - videoconference
    - audioconference
    - email
    - secure text messaging
  - Routing/triage functionality – the telehealth platform enables patients to identify an appropriate, networked team of care providers
  - SDKs and APIs that enable telehealth applications to interface with patient monitoring devices
  - Patient monitoring devices that send telemetry data via the home monitoring device
    - blood pressure
    - heart monitoring
    - BMI / weight scales
    - other telemetry devices, as appropriate
  - Home monitoring device (e.g., specialized mobile application, standalone device) that transmits telemetry data to the telehealth platform and provides video connectivity

Components for Remote/Patient Home Environment

- **Personal firewall** – an application that controls network traffic to and from a computer, permitting or denying communications based on a security policy
- **Wireless access point router** – a device that performs the functions of a router and includes the functions of a wireless access point
- **Endpoint protection (anti-malware)** – a type of software program designed to prevent, detect, and remove malicious software (malware) on information technology (IT) systems and on individual computing devices
- **Cable modem** – a device that provides a demarcation point for cable access and presents an Ethernet interface to allow internet access via the cable infrastructure

- **Wireless router** – a device that provides wireless connectivity to the home network and provides access to the internet via a connection to the cable modem
- **Telehealth application** – an application residing on a managed or unmanaged mobile device or on a specialized standalone device, that facilitates the transmission of telemetry data, and video connectivity, between the patient and HDO
- **Patient monitoring device** – a peripheral device used by the patient to perform diagnostic tasks (e.g., measure blood pressure, glucose levels, and BMI/weight) and to send the telemetry data via Bluetooth or wireless connectivity to the telehealth application

Components for HDO Environment

- **Network access control** – discovers and accurately identifies devices connected to wired networks, wireless networks, and VPNs, and provides network access controls to ensure that only authorized individuals with authorized devices can access the systems and data that access policy permits
- **Network firewall** – a network security device that monitors and controls incoming and outgoing network traffic, based on defined security rules
- **Intrusion Detection System (IDS) (host/network)** – a device or software application that monitors a network or systems for malicious activity or policy violations
- **Intrusion Prevention System (IPS)** – a device that monitors network traffic and can take immediate action, such as shutting down a port, based on a set of rules established by the network administrator
- **VPN** – a secure endpoint access solution that delivers secure remote access through virtual private networking
- **Governance, Risk, and Compliance (GRC) tool** – automated management for an organization's overall governance, enterprise risk management, and compliance with regulations
- **Network management tool** – provides server, application-management, and monitoring services, as well as asset life-cycle management
- **Endpoint protection and security** – provides server hardening, protection, monitoring, and workload micro-segmentation for private cloud and physical on-premises data-center environments, along with support for containers, and provides full-disk and removable media encryption
- **Anti-ransomware** – helps enterprises defend against ransomware attacks by exposing, detecting, and quarantining advanced and evasive ransomware
- **Application security scanning/testing** – provides a means for custom application code testing (static/dynamic)

DRAFT

Desired Security Characteristics

The primary security functions and processes to be implemented for this project are listed below and are based on NIST Cybersecurity Framework Version 1.1.

IDENTIFY (ID) – *These activities are foundational to developing an organizational understanding to manage risk.*

- **Asset management** – includes the identification and management of assets on the network, and the management of the assets to be deployed to equipment. Implementation of this category may vary depending on the parties managing the equipment. However, this category remains relevant as a fundamental component in establishing appropriate cybersecurity practices.
- **Governance** – Organizational cybersecurity policy is established and communicated. Governance practices are appropriate for HDOs and their business associates (BAs), including technology providers, such as those vendors that develop, support, and operate telehealth platforms.
- **Risk assessment** – includes the risk management strategy. Risk assessment is a fundamental component for HDOs and their BAs.
- **Supply chain risk management** – The nature of telehealth with RPM is that the system integrates components sourced from disparate vendors and may involve relationships established with multiple suppliers, including cloud services providers.

PROTECT (PR) – *These activities support the ability to develop and implement appropriate safeguards based on risk.*

- **Identity management, authentication, and access control** – includes user account management and remote access
  - controlling (and auditing) user accounts
  - controlling (and auditing) access by external users
  - enforcing least privilege for all (internal and external) users
  - enforcing separation-of-duties policies
    - privileged access management (PAM) with an emphasis on the separation of duties
  - enforcing least functionality
- **Data security** – includes data confidentiality, integrity, and availability
  - securing and monitoring the storage of data – includes data encryption (for data at rest)
    - access control on data
    - data-at-rest controls should implement some form of a data security manager that would allow for policy application to encrypted data, inclusive of access control policy
  - securing the distribution of data – includes data encryption (for data in transit) and a data loss prevention mechanism
  - controls that promote data integrity

- cryptographic modules validated as meeting NIST Federal Information Processing Standard (FIPS) 140-2 are preferred
- physical security provided by an access-controlled data center to host the third-party telehealth servers and storage
- **Information protection processes and procedures** – includes data backup and endpoint protection
- **Maintenance** – includes local and remote maintenance
- **Protective technology** – host-based intrusion prevention, solutions for malware (malicious-code detection), audit logging, (automated) audit log review, and physical protection

DETECT (DE) – *enables the timely discovery of a cybersecurity event*

- **Security continuous monitoring** – monitoring for unauthorized personnel, devices, software, and connections
  - vulnerability management – includes vulnerability scanning and remediation
  - patch management
  - system configuration security settings
  - user account usage (local and remote) and user behavioral analytics

RESPOND (RS) – *the ability to develop and implement activities designed to contain the impact of a detected cybersecurity event*

- **Response planning** – Response processes and procedures are executed and maintained to ensure a response to a detected cybersecurity incident.
- **Mitigation** – Activities are performed to prevent the expansion of a cybersecurity event, mitigate its effects, and resolve the incident.

RECOVER (RC) – *the ability to develop and implement activities that support the timely recovery of normal operations after a cybersecurity incident*

- **Recovery planning** – Recovery processes and procedures are executed and maintained to ensure the restoration of systems or assets affected by cybersecurity incidents.
- **Communications** – Restoration activities are coordinated with internal and external parties (e.g., coordinating centers, internet service providers, owners of attacking systems, victims, other computer security incident response teams, vendors).

4 RELEVANT STANDARDS AND GUIDANCE

General Cybersecurity and Risk Management:

- Association for Advancement of Medical Instrumentation (AAMI) Technical Information Report (TIR)57, "Principles for medical device security – Risk management"
- International Organization for Standardization (ISO) / International Electrotechnical Commission (IEC) Standard 27001:2013, *Information technology – Security techniques – Information security management systems – Requirements*
- American National Standards Institute (ANSI)/AAMI/IEC Standard 80001-1:2010, *Application of risk management for IT-networks incorporating medical devices – Part 1: Roles, responsibilities and activities*

- IEC Technical Report (TR) 80001-2-1 Edition 1.0 2012-07, "Application of risk management for IT-networks incorporating medical devices – Part 2-1: Step-by-step risk management of medical IT-networks – Practical applications and examples"

- IEC TR 80001-2-2 Edition 1.0 2012-07, "Application of risk management for IT-networks incorporating medical devices – Part 2-2: Guidance for the disclosure and communication of medical device security needs, risks and controls"

- "Framework for Improving Critical Infrastructure Cybersecurity" (NIST Cybersecurity Framework) Version 1.1
  https://www.nist.gov/cyberframework/framework

- NIST Special Publication (SP) 800-30 Revision 1, "Guide for Conducting Risk Assessments"
  http://nvlpubs.nist.gov/nistpubs/Legacy/SP/nistspecialpublication800-30r1.pdf

- NIST SP 800-37 Revision 1, "Guide for Applying the Risk Management Framework to Federal Information Systems: A Security Life Cycle Approach"
  http://nvlpubs.nist.gov/nistpubs/SpecialPublications/NIST.SP.800-37r1.pdf

- NIST SP 800-39, "Managing Information Security Risk: Organization, Mission, and Information System View"
  http://nvlpubs.nist.gov/nistpubs/Legacy/SP/nistspecialpublication800-39.pdf

- NIST SP 800-53 Revision 4, "Security and Privacy Controls for Federal Information Systems and Organizations"
  http://nvlpubs.nist.gov/nistpubs/SpecialPublications/NIST.SP.800-53r4.pdf

Cybersecurity/Technology-Related Standards:

- NIST FIPS 140-2, *Security Requirements for Cryptographic Modules*
  https://csrc.nist.gov/publications/detail/fips/140/2/final

- NIST SP 800-41 Revision 1, "Guidelines on Firewalls and Firewall Policy"
  http://nvlpubs.nist.gov/nistpubs/Legacy/SP/nistspecialpublication800-41r1.pdf

- NIST SP 800-52 Revision 1, "Guidelines for the Selection, Configuration, and Use of Transport Layer Security (TLS) Implementations"
  http://nvlpubs.nist.gov/nistpubs/SpecialPublications/NIST.SP.800-52r1.pdf

- NIST SP 800-57 Part 1 Revision 4, "Recommendation for Key Management: Part 1: General"
  http://nvlpubs.nist.gov/nistpubs/SpecialPublications/NIST.SP.800-57pt1r4.pdf

- NIST SP 800-77, "Guide to IPsec VPNs"
  http://nvlpubs.nist.gov/nistpubs/Legacy/SP/nistspecialpublication800-77.pdf

- NIST SP 800-95, "Guide to Secure Web Services"
  http://nvlpubs.nist.gov/nistpubs/Legacy/SP/nistspecialpublication800-95.pdf

- NIST SP 800-144, "Guidelines on Security and Privacy in Public Cloud Computing"
  http://nvlpubs.nist.gov/nistpubs/Legacy/SP/nistspecialpublication800-144.pdf

- NIST SP 800-146, "Cloud Computing Synopsis and Recommendations"
  http://nvlpubs.nist.gov/nistpubs/Legacy/SP/nistspecialpublication800-146.pdf

- Draft NIST SP 800-121 Revision 2, "Guide to Bluetooth Security"
  https://csrc.nist.gov/csrc/media/publications/sp/800-121/rev-2/draft/documents/sp800_121_r2_draft.pdf

- NIST SP 1800-1, "Securing Electronic Health Records on Mobile Devices"
  https://csrc.nist.gov/publications/detail/sp/1800-1/final

Other Relevant Regulations, Standards, and Guidance (Healthcare/Medical Devices):

- Department of Health and Human Services Office for Civil Rights, "HIPAA Security Rule Crosswalk to NIST Cybersecurity Framework"
  https://www.hhs.gov/sites/default/files/nist-csf-to-hipaa-security-rule-crosswalk-02-22-2016-final.pdf

- Department of Homeland Security, "Attack Surface: Healthcare and Public Health Sector"
  https://info.publicintelligence.net/NCCIC-MedicalDevices.pdf

- Food and Drug Administration (FDA), "Content of Premarket Submissions for Management of Cybersecurity in Medical Devices: Guidance for Industry and Food and Drug Administration Staff"
  https://www.fda.gov/downloads/medicaldevices/deviceregulationandguidance/guidancedocuments/ucm356190.pdf

- FDA, "Guidance for Industry: Cybersecurity for Networked Medical Devices Containing Off-the-Shelf (OTS) Software"
  https://www.fda.gov/downloads/MedicalDevices/DeviceRegulationandGuidance/GuidanceDocuments/UCM077823.pdf

- FDA, "Postmarket Management of Cybersecurity in Medical Devices: Guidance for Industry and Food and Drug Administration Staff"
  https://www.fda.gov/ucm/groups/fdagov-public/@fdagov-meddev-gen/documents/document/ucm482022.pdf

- NIST SP 800-66 Revision 1: "An Introductory Resource Guide for Implementing the Health Insurance Portability and Accountability Act (HIPAA) Security Rule"
  http://nvlpubs.nist.gov/nistpubs/Legacy/SP/nistspecialpublication800-66r1.pdf

5   SECURITY CONTROL MAP

Table 5-1 maps the characteristics of the commercial products that the NCCoE will apply to this cybersecurity challenge to the applicable standards and best practices described in the Framework for Improving Critical Infrastructure Cybersecurity (NIST Cybersecurity Framework), and the healthcare-sector specific standards and guidance, such as IEC TR 80001-2-2, HIPAA, and ISO/IEC 27001. This exercise is meant to demonstrate the real-world applicability of standards and best practices, but does not imply that products with these characteristics will meet your industry's requirements for regulatory approval or accreditation.

DRAFT

Table 5-1: Security Control Map

| Function | NIST Cybersecurity Framework Version 1.1 | | NIST SP 800-53 Revision 4 | Sector-Specific Standards and Best Practices | | |
	Category	Subcategory		IEC TR 80001-2-2	HIPAA Security Rule	ISO/IEC 27001
IDENTIFY (ID)	Asset Management (ID.AM)	ID.AM-1: Physical devices and systems within the organization are inventoried.	CM-8	Not applicable	45 C.F.R. §§ 164.308(a)(1)(ii)(A), 164.310(a)(2)(ii), 164.310(d)	A.8.1.1, A.8.1.2
		ID.AM-5: Resources (e.g., hardware, devices, data, time, and software) are prioritized based on their classification, criticality, and business value.	CP-2, RA-2, SA-14	DTBK	45 C.F.R. § 164.308(a)(7)(ii)(E)	A.8.2.1
	Risk Assessment (ID.RA)	ID.RA-1: Asset vulnerabilities are identified and documented.	CA-2, CA-7, CA-8, RA-3, RA-5, SA-5, SA-11, SI-2, SI-4, SI-5	RDMP	45 C.F.R. §§ 164.308(a)(1)(ii)(A), 164.308(a)(7)(ii)(E), 164.308(a)(8), 164.310(a)(1), 164.312(a)(1), 164.316(b)(2)(iii)	A.12.6.1, A.18.2.3
		ID.RA-4: Potential business impacts and likelihoods are identified.	RA-2, RA-3, PM-9, PM-11, SA-14	SAHD, SGUD	45 C.F.R. §§ 164.308(a)(1)(i), 164.308(a)(1)(ii)(A), 164.308(a)(1)(ii)(B), 164.308(a)(6), 164.308(a)(7)(ii)(E), 164.308(a)(8), 164.316(a)	A.12.6.1, A.18.2.3

NIST Cybersecurity Framework Version 1.1			NIST SP 800-53 Revision 4	Sector-Specific Standards and Best Practices		
Function	**Category**	**Subcategory**		**IEC TR 80001-2-2**	**HIPAA Security Rule**	**ISO/IEC 27001**
		ID.RA-5: Threats, vulnerabilities, likelihoods, and impacts are used to determine risk.	RA-2, RA-3, PM-16	SGUD	45 C.F.R. §§ 164.308(a)(1)(ii)(A), 164.308(a)(1)(ii)(B), 164.308(a)(1)(ii)(D), 164.308(a)(7)(ii)(D), 164.308(a)(7)(ii)(E), 164.316(a)	None
		ID.RA-6: Risk responses are identified and prioritized.	PM-4, PM-9	DTBK, SGUD	45 C.F.R. §§ 164.308(a)(1)(ii)(B), 164.314(a)(2)(i)(C), 164.314(b)(2)(iv)	None
		(Note: not directly mapped in CSF)	AC-1, AC-11, AC-12	ALOF	Not applicable	None
PROTECT (PR)	Identity Management and Access Control (PR.AC)	PR.AC-1: Identities and credentials are issued, managed, revoked, and audited for authorized devices, users, and processes.	AC-2, IA Family	AUTH, CNFS, EMRG, PAUT	45 C.F.R. §§ 164.308(a)(3)(ii)(B), 164.308(a)(3)(ii)(C), 164.308(a)(4)(i), 164.308(a)(4)(ii)(B), 164.308(a)(4)(ii)(C), 164.312(a)(2)(i), 164.312(a)(2)(ii), 164.312(a)(2)(iii), 164.312(d)	A.9.2.1, A.9.2.2, A.9.2.4, A.9.3.1, A.9.4.2, A.9.4.3

NIST Cybersecurity Framework Version 1.1				Sector-Specific Standards and Best Practices		
Function	Category	Subcategory	NIST SP 800-53 Revision 4	IEC TR 80001-2-2	HIPAA Security Rule	ISO/IEC 27001
		PR.AC-2: Physical access to assets is managed and protected.	PE-2, PE-3, PE-4, PE-5, PE-6, PE-9	PLOK, TXCF, TXIG	45 C.F.R. §§ 164.308(a)(1)(ii)(B), 164.308(a)(7)(i), 164.308(a)(7)(ii)(A), 164.310(a)(1), 164.310(a)(2)(i), 164.310(a)(2)(ii), 164.310(a)(2)(iii), 164.310(b), 164.310(c), 164.310(d)(1), 164.310(d)(2)(iii)	A.11.1.1, A.11.1.2, A.11.1.4, A.11.1.6, A.11.2.3
		PR.AC-3: Remote access is managed.	AC-17, AC-19, AC-20	NAUT, PAUT	45 C.F.R. §§ 164.308(a)(4)(i), 164.308(b)(1), 164.308(b)(3), 164.310(b), 164.312(e)(1), 164.312(e)(2)(ii)	A.6.2.2, A.13.1.1, A.13.2.1
		PR.AC-4: Access permissions and authorizations are managed, incorporating the principles of least privilege and separation of duties.	AC-2, AC-3, AC-5, AC-6, AC-16	AUTH, CNFS, EMRG, NAUT, PAUT	45 C.F.R. §§ 164.308(a)(3), 164.308(a)(4), 164.310(a)(2)(iii), 164.310(b), 164.312(a)(1), 164.312(a)(2)(i), 164.312(a)(2)(ii)	A.6.1.2, A.9.1.2, A.9.2.3, A.9.4.1, A.9.4.4

NIST Cybersecurity Framework Version 1.1				Sector-Specific Standards and Best Practices		
Function	Category	Subcategory	NIST SP 800-53 Revision 4	IEC TR 80001-2-2	HIPAA Security Rule	ISO/IEC 27001
		PR.AC-5: Network integrity is protected, incorporating network segregation where appropriate.	AC-4, SC-7	NAUT	45 C.F.R. §§ 164.308(a)(4)(ii)(B), 164.310(a)(1), 164.310(b), 164.312(a)(1), 164.312(b), 164.312(c), 164.312(e)	A.13.1.1, A.13.1.3, A.13.2.1
		PR.AC-6: Identities are proofed and bound to credentials, and asserted in interactions when appropriate.	AC-2, AC-3, AC-5, AC-6, AC-16, AC-19, AC-24, IA-2, IA-4, IA-5, IA-8, PE-2, PS-3	AUTH, CNFS, EMRG, NAUT, PLOK, SGUD	Not applicable	A.6.1.2, A.7.1.1, A.9.1.2, A.9.2.2, A.9.2.3, A.9.2.5, A.9.2.6, A.9.4.1, A.9.4.4
	Data Security (PR.DS)	PR.DS-1: Data at rest is protected.	SC-28	IGAU, STCF	45 C.F.R. §§ 164.308(a)(1)(ii)(D), 164.308(b)(1), 164.310(d), 164.312(a)(1), 164.312(a)(2)(iii), 164.312(a)(2)(iv), 164.312(b), 164.312(c), 164.312(d), 164.314(b)(2)(i)	A.8.2.3

NIST Cybersecurity Framework Version 1.1			Sector-Specific Standards and Best Practices		
Function	Category	Subcategory	NIST SP 800-53 Revision 4	IEC TR 80001-2-2	HIPAA Security Rule	ISO/IEC 27001
		PR.DS-2: Data in transit is protected.	SC-8	IGAU, TXCF	45 C.F.R. §§ 164.308(b)(1), 164.308(b)(2), 164.312(e)(1), 164.312(e)(2)(i), 164.312(e)(2)(ii), 164.314(b)(2)(i)	A.8.2.3, A.13.1.1, A.13.2.1, A.13.2.3, A.14.1.2, A.14.1.3
		PR.DS-3: Assets are formally managed throughout removal, transfers, and disposition.	CM-8, MP-6, PE-16	Not applicable	45 C.F.R. §§ 164.308(a)(1)(ii)(A), 164.310(a)(2)(ii), 164.310(a)(2)(iii), 164.310(a)(2)(iv), 164.310(d)(1), 164.310(d)(2)	A.12.3.1
		PR.DS-4: Adequate capacity to ensure availability is maintained.	AU-4, CP-2, SC-5	AUDT, DTBK	45 C.F.R. §§ 164.308(a)(1)(ii)(A), 164.308(a)(1)(ii)(B), 164.308(a)(7), 164.310(a)(2)(i), 164.310(d)(2)(iv), 164.312(a)(2)(ii)	A.12.3.1

	NIST Cybersecurity Framework Version 1.1			Sector-Specific Standards and Best Practices		
Function	**Category**	**Subcategory**	**NIST SP 800-53 Revision 4**	**IEC TR 80001-2-2**	**HIPAA Security Rule**	**ISO/IEC 27001**
		PR.DS-5: Protections against data leaks are implemented.	AC-4, AC-5, AC-6, PE-19, PS-3, PS-6, SC-7, SC-8, SC-13, SC-31, SI-4	AUTH, CNFS, STCF, TXCF, TXIG	45 C.F.R. §§ 164.308(a)(1)(ii)(D), 164.308(a)(3), 164.308(a)(4), 164.310(b), 164.310(c), 164.312(a), 164.312(e)	A.6.1.2, A.7.1.1, A.7.1.2, A.7.3.1, A.8.2.2, A.8.2.3, A.9.1.1, A.9.1.2, A.9.2.3, A.9.4.1, A.9.4.4, A.9.4.5, A.13.1.3, A.13.2.1, A.13.2.3, A.13.2.4, A.14.1.2, A.14.1.3
		PR.DS-6: Integrity checking mechanisms are used to verify software, firmware, and information integrity.	SI-7	IGAU	45 C.F.R. §§ 164.308(a)(1)(ii)(D), 164.312(b), 164.312(c)(1), 164.312(c)(2), 164.312(e)(2)(i)	A.12.2.1, A.12.5.1, A.14.1.2, A.14.1.3
		PR.DS-7: The development and testing environment(s) are separate from the production environment.	CM-2	CNFS	45 C.F.R. § 164.308(a)(4)	A.12.1.4
	Information Protection Processes and Procedures (PR.IP)	PR.IP-4: Backups of information are conducted, maintained, and tested periodically.	CP-4, CP-6, CP-9	DTBK	45 C.F.R. §§ 164.308(a)(7)(ii)(A), 164.308(a)(7)(ii)(B), 164.308(a)(7)(ii)(D), 164.310(a)(2)(i), 164.310(d)(2)(iv)	A.12.3.1, A.17.1.2, A.17.1.3, A.18.1.3

NIST Cybersecurity Framework Version 1.1				Sector-Specific Standards and Best Practices		
Function	Category	Subcategory	NIST SP 800-53 Revision 4	IEC TR 80001-2-2	HIPAA Security Rule	ISO/IEC 27001
		PR.IP-6: Data is destroyed according to policy.	MP-6	DIDT	45 C.F.R. §§ 164.310(d)(2)(i), 164.310(d)(2)(ii)	A.8.2.3, A.8.3.1, A.8.3.2, A.11.2.7
		PR.IP-9: Response plans (Incident Response and Business Continuity) and recovery plans (Incident Recovery and Disaster Recovery) are in place and managed.	CP-2, IR-8	DTBK	45 C.F.R. §§ 164.308(a)(6), 164.308(a)(7), 164.310(a)(2)(i), 164.312(a)(2)(ii)	A.16.1.1, A.17.1.1, A.17.1.2
		PR.IP-10: Response and recovery plans are tested.	CP-4, IR-3, PM-14	DTBK	45 C.F.R. § 164.308(a)(7)(ii)(D)	A.17.1.3
		PR.IP-12: A vulnerability management plan is developed and implemented.	RA-3, RA-5, SI-2	MLDP	45 C.F.R. §§ 164.308(a)(1)(i), 164.308(a)(1)(ii)(A), 164.308(a)(1)(ii)(B)	A.12.6.1, A.18.2.2
	Maintenance (PR.MA)	PR.MA-1: Maintenance and repair of organizational assets is performed and logged in a timely manner, with approved and controlled tools.	MA-2, MA-3, MA-5	CSUP, RDMP	45 C.F.R. §§ 164.308(a)(3)(ii)(A), 164.310(a)(2)(iv)	A.11.1.2, A.11.2.4, A.11.2.5

NIST Cybersecurity Framework Version 1.1				Sector-Specific Standards and Best Practices		
Function	Category	Subcategory	NIST SP 800-53 Revision 4	IEC TR 80001-2-2	HIPAA Security Rule	ISO/IEC 27001
		PR.MA-2: Remote maintenance of organizational assets is approved, logged, and performed in a manner that prevents unauthorized access.	MA-4	CSUP	45 C.F.R. §§ 164.308(a)(1)(ii)(D), 164.308(a)(3)(ii)(A), 164.310(d)(1), 164.310(d)(2)(ii), 164.310(d)(2)(iii), 164.312(a), 164.312(a)(2)(ii), 164.312(a)(2)(iv), 164.312(b), 164.312(d), 164.312(e)	A.11.2.4, A.15.1.1, A.15.2.1
		PR.PT-1: Audit/log records are determined, documented, implemented, and reviewed in accordance with policy.	AC-4, AC-17, AC-18, CP-8, SC-7	AUDT	45 C.F.R. §§ 164.308(a)(1)(ii)(D), 164.308(a)(5)(ii)(C), 164.310(a)(2)(iv), 164.310(d)(2)(iii), 164.312(b)	A.12.4.1, A.12.4.2, A.12.4.3, A.12.4.4, A.12.7.1
	Protective Technology (PR.PT)	PR.PT-3: The principle of least functionality is incorporated by configuring systems to provide only essential capabilities.	AC-3, CM-7	AUTH, CNFS	45 C.F.R. §§ 164.308(a)(3), 164.308(a)(4), 164.310(a)(2)(iii), 164.310(b), 164.310(c), 164.312(a)(1), 164.312(a)(2)(i), 164.312(a)(2)(ii), 164.312(a)(2)(iv)	A.9.1.2

NIST Cybersecurity Framework Version 1.1			NIST SP 800-53 Revision 4	Sector-Specific Standards and Best Practices		
Function	Category	Subcategory		IEC TR 80001-2-2	HIPAA Security Rule	ISO/IEC 27001
		PR.PT-4: Communications and control networks are protected.	AC-4, AC-17, AC-18, CP-8, SC-7	DTBK	45 C.F.R. §§ 164.308(a)(1)(ii)(D), 164.312(a)(1), 164.312(b), 164.312(e)	A.13.1.1, A.13.2.1
DETECT (DE)	Anomalies and Events (DE.AE)	DE.AE-1: A baseline of network operations and expected data flows for users and systems is established and managed.	AC-4, CA-3, CM-2, SI-4	AUTH, CNFS	45 C.F.R. §§ 164.308(a)(1)(ii)(D), 164.312(b)	None
		DE.AE-2: Detected events are analyzed to understand attack targets and methods.	CP-2, IR-4, RA-3, SI-4	DTBK	45 C.F.R. § 164.308(6)(i)	A.16.1.1, A.16.1.4
	Security Continuous Monitoring (DE.CM)	DE.CM-1: The network is monitored to detect potential cybersecurity events.	AC-2, AU-12, CA-7, CM-3, SC-5, SC-7, SI-4	AUTH, CNFS, EMRG, MLDP	45 C.F.R. §§ 164.308(a)(1)(ii)(D), 164.308(a)(5)(ii)(B), 164.308(a)(5)(ii)(C), 164.308(a)(8), 164.312(b), 164.312(e)(2)(i)	None
		DE.CM-2: The physical environment is monitored to detect potential cybersecurity events.	CA-7, PE-3, PE-6, PE-20	MLDP	45 C.F.R. §§ 164.310(a)(2)(ii), 164.310(a)(2)(iii)	None
		DE.CM-4: Malicious code is detected.	SI-3	IGAU, MLDP, TXIG	45 C.F.R. §§ 164.308(a)(1)(ii)(D), 164.308(a)(5)(ii)(B)	A.12.2.1

DRAFT

| Function | NIST Cybersecurity Framework Version 1.1 | | Sector-Specific Standards and Best Practices | | | |
	Category	Subcategory	NIST SP 800-53 Revision 4	IEC TR 80001-2-2	HIPAA Security Rule	ISO/IEC 27001
		DE.CM-6: External service provider activity is monitored to detect potential cybersecurity events.	CA-7, PS-7, SA-4, SA-9, SI-4	RDMP	45 C.F.R. § 164.308(a)(1)(ii)(D)	A.14.2.7, A.15.2.1
		DE.CM-7: Monitoring for unauthorized personnel, connections, devices, and software is performed.	AU-12, CA-7, CM-3, CM-8, PE-3, PE-6, PE-20, SI-4	AUDT, CNFS, PAUT, PLOK, MLDP, NAUT, SGUD	45 C.F.R. §§ 164.308(a)(1)(ii)(D), 164.308(a)(5)(ii)(B), 164.308(a)(5)(ii)(C), 164.310(a)(1), 164.310(a)(2)(ii), 164.310(a)(2)(iii), 164.310(b), 164.310(c), 164.310(d)(1), 164.310(d)(2)(iii), 164.312(b), 164.314(b)(2)(i)	None
		DE.CM-8: Vulnerability scans are performed.	RA-5	MLDP	45 C.F.R. §§ 164.308(a)(1)(i), 164.308(a)(8)	A.12.6.1
RESPOND (RS)	Response Planning (RS.RP)	RS.RP-1: Response plan is executed during or after an event.	CP-2, CP-10, IR-4, IR-8	DTBK, SGUD, MLDP	45 C.F.R. §§ 164.308(a)(6)(ii), 164.308(a)(7)(i), 164.308(a)(7)(ii)(A), 164.308(a)(7)(ii)(B), 164.308(a)(7)(ii)(C), 164.310(a)(2)(i), 164.312(a)(2)(ii)	A.16.1.5

Project Description: Securing Telehealth Remote Patient Monitoring Ecosystem   23

DRAFT

NIST Cybersecurity Framework Version 1.1			Sector-Specific Standards and Best Practices			
Function	**Category**	**Subcategory**	**NIST SP 800-53 Revision 4**	**IEC TR 80001-2-2**	**HIPAA Security Rule**	**ISO/IEC 27001**
	Improvements (RS.IM)	RS.IM-1: Response plans incorporate lessons learned.	CP-2, IR-4, IR-8	DTBK	45 C.F.R. §§ 164.308(a)(7)(ii)(D), 164.308(a)(8), 164.316(b)(2)(iii)	A.16.1.6
		RS.IM-2: Response strategies are updated.	CP-2, IR-4, IR-8	DTBK	45 C.F.R. §§ 164.308(a)(7)(ii)(D), 164.308(a)(8)	None
RECOVER (RC)	Recovery Planning (RC.RP)	RC.RP-1: Recovery plan is executed during or after an event.	CP-10, IR-4, IR-8	DTBK	45 C.F.R. §§ 164.308(a)(7), 164.310(a)(2)(i)	A.16.1.5

APPENDIX A REFERENCES

[1] Foley & Lardner LLP, "2017 telemedicine and digital health survey: Telemedicine surges ahead as providers, patients embrace technology," 2017.
Available: https://www.foley.com/files/uploads/2017-Telemedicine-Survey-Report-11-8-17.pdf.

[2] Maryland Health Care Commission, "Remote patient monitoring telehealth grants: Brief and final reports," Mar. 2017.
Available: http://mhcc.maryland.gov/mhcc/pages/hit/hit_telemedicine/documents/Telehealth_Brief_Reports_FINAL_031617.pdf.

[3] G. O'Brien et al., "Securing electronic health records on mobile devices," NIST, Gaithersburg, MD, NIST SP 1800-1, Jul. 2018.
Available: https://www.nccoe.nist.gov/sites/default/files/library/sp1800/hit-ehr-nist-sp1800-1.pdf.

[4] G. O'Brien et al., "Securing wireless infusion pumps in healthcare delivery organizations," NIST, Gaithersburg, MD, NIST SP 1800-8, Aug. 2018.
Available: https://www.nccoe.nist.gov/sites/default/files/library/sp1800/hit-wip-nist-sp1800-8.pdf.

APPENDIX B ACRONYMS AND ABBREVIATIONS

AAMI	Association for Advancement of Medical Instrumentation
ANSI	American National Standards Institute
API	Application Programming Interface
BA	Business Associate
BMI	Body Mass Index
CFR	Code of Federal Regulations
DE	Detect
FDA	Food and Drug Administration
FIPS	Federal Information Processing Standard
GRC	Governance, Risk, and Compliance
HDO	Health Delivery Organization
ID	Identify
IdAM	Identity and Access Management
IDS	Intrusion Detection System
IEC	International Electrotechnical Commission
IPS	Intrusion Prevention System
ISO	International Organization for Standardization
IT	Information Technology
NCCoE	National Cybersecurity Center of Excellence
NIST	National Institute of Standards and Technology
PAM	Privileged Access Management
PR	Protect
RC	Recover
RPM	Remote Patient Monitoring
RS	Respond
SaaS	Software as a Service
SDK	Software Development Kit
SP	Special Publication
TIR	Technical Information Report
TR	Technical Report
VPN	Virtual Private Network

www.ingramcontent.com/pod-product-compliance
Lightning Source LLC
LaVergne TN
LVHW060202050326
832903LV00016B/350